Automated Security Testing

Tools and Techniques for Protecting Web Applications

Table of Contents

1. Introduction 1

2. Introduction to Automated Security Testing 2

    2.1. What is Automation? 2

    2.2. What is Security Testing? 2

    2.3. Need for Automated Security Testing 3

    2.4. How Does Automated Security Testing Work? 3

    2.5. Understanding Common Vulnerabilities and Exposures
(CVEs) 4

    2.6. The Importance of a Multidimensional Approach 5

3. Understanding Web Application Vulnerabilities 6

    3.1. Types of Web Application Vulnerabilities and Their
Exploitation 6

    3.2. Mitigating Web Application Vulnerabilities 7

    3.3. Policy Considerations 8

4. Essentials of Security Testing: Tools and Techniques 9

    4.1. Understanding Web Application Security 9

    4.2. Common Web Application Vulnerabilities 9

    4.3. Tools for Web Application Security Testing 10

    4.4. Techniques for Security Testing 11

    4.5. Formulating a Security Testing Strategy 12

    4.6. Keeping up with Regulation Changes 12

5. Delving into Automated Security Testing Tools 14

    5.1. Understanding Automated Security Testing Tools 14

    5.2. Choosing the Right Tool 15

    5.3. Most Popular Automated Security Testing Tools 15

    5.4. The advantages and disadvantages of automated security
testing tools 16

    5.5. The Importance of Manual Penetration Testing 16

5.6. Integrating Automated Security Tools into your SDLC 17

6. Proactive Defense: Implementing Regular Automated Tests 18

    6.1. Benefit of Regular Automated Tests 18

    6.2. Overview of Automated Security Testing 18

    6.3. Setting up a Testing Environment 19

    6.4. Implementing and Scheduling Regular Tests 19

    6.5. Reacting to Test Results 20

    6.6. The Need for Continuous Improvement 20

    6.7. Conclusion 21

7. Case Study: Success Stories of Automated Security Testing 22

    7.1. Automating Security at Acme Corp 22

    7.2. Improving Efficiency at BigSoftware Inc 23

    7.3. Cybertech Pvt Ltd: Balancing Human and Machine 23

    7.4. Securing Startup Terrain: AlphaStart 24

8. Walking Through Web Application Security Coding Practices 26

    8.1. Why Code Secure Web Applications? 26

    8.2. Secure Coding Techniques 26

    8.3. Language-Specific Practices 27

    8.4. Building Security Touchpoints 27

    8.5. Awareness and Training 28

9. Threat Modelling: Anticipating Cybersecurity Challenges 29

10. Overview of Threat Modeling 30

    10.1. Threat Modeling Process 30

    10.2. Advantages of Threat Modeling 31

11. Steps in Threat Modeling 32

    11.1. Identify Security Objectives 32

    11.2. Create a Detailed Application Overview 32

    11.3. Identify and Analyze Threats 33

    11.4. Prioritize and Respond to Threats 33

    11.5. Validate, Monitor, and Iterate 33

12. Threat Modeling Tools 35

13. Conclusion 36

14. From Reactive to Proactive: Developing an Effective Security
Testing Strategy 37

    14.1. The Proactive Approach: A Paradigm Shift 37

    14.2. The Merits of Proactive Testing 38

    14.3. The Reactive Method: A Study 38

    14.4. Leveraging Automated Tools for Proactive Security 38

    14.5. Develop a Risk-Based Strategy 39

    14.6. Cultivate an Organizational Culture around Proactive
Security 39

    14.7. Integrating Security into the Development Lifecycle 40

    14.8. Continual Learning and Improvement 40

    14.9. Conclusion 40

15. Future Trends in Automated Security Testing 42

    15.1. The Surge of AI and Machine Learning 42

    15.2. Continuous and Comprehensive Testing 42

    15.3. Integration of Tools 43

    15.4. Increased Usage of Blockchain 43

    15.5. Rise of User Behavior Analytics 44

    15.6. The Evolution of Risk-Based Testing 44

Chapter 1. Introduction

In today's digital age where web applications are pervasive and vital, effective protection of these platforms is paramount. Our Special Report on "Automated Security Testing: Tools and Techniques for Protecting Web Applications" is designed to lend a hand in this exact realm. This crucial resource will guide you through the nuances of automated security testing, presenting pertinent tools and techniques in an accessible, down-to-earth manner. It doesn't matter if you are experienced in web application security or just getting started; this comprehensive guide has something for everyone. It endeavors to demystify the complex world of website protection, bringing you valuable knowledge to safeguard your web applications effectively. No jargon, no unnecessary complexity, just practical and relevant insights to fortify your digital assets. Don't miss out on your chance to stay ahead in the ever-advancing field of web application security. Secure your copy today and pave the way for a safer web tomorrow.

Chapter 2. Introduction to Automated Security Testing

As the digital landscape continues to grow, our reliance on web applications has seamlessly integrated with our everyday lives. As such, the need for robust security measures to protect these digital transactions is both vital and non-negotiable. At the heart of this protection lies the bedrock of automated security testing, a method used to ensure the fortification of web applications against potential cyberattacks.

To facilitate a clear understanding, let's break down the two key terms - 'Automation' and 'Security Testing'.

2.1. What is Automation?

In simple terms, automation is the technology by which a process or procedure is performed with minimal human assistance. This not only enhances efficiency but also ensures precision and consistency in tasks that may otherwise be prone to human error. In the realm of digital security, this translates to deploying software tools that can uncover potential vulnerabilities within your web applications.

2.2. What is Security Testing?

Security testing, an aspect of software testing, aims to reveal system vulnerabilities, threats, risks that could affect its data security and divulge valuable information to unauthorized or malicious entities. This testing type targets to unearth any potential flaws and weaknesses in the security mechanism of a web application that could result in a loss of data, revenue, reputation, and even trust.

By combining these concepts, we find ourselves in the sphere of

Automated Security Testing, which aims to identify vulnerabilities in the system without manual intervention. But why do we need automated security testing for web applications?

2.3. Need for Automated Security Testing

Securing a web application is a continuous journey, not a one-time event. New vulnerabilities surface every day, and attackers constantly innovate their strategies. Hence, the process of auditing needs to be ongoing, which is where automated security testing enters. It allows for regular, uniform, and far-reaching testing, ensuring that no stone remains unturned in the quest for cyber-resilience.

Continuous Integration & Continuous Delivery (CI/CD) pipeline has today become an indispensable part of modern software development process making automation an even more important aspect. With thousands of lines of codes being written and deployed daily, it's an impossible feat to manually check each one for potential vulnerabilities. An automated solution significantly enhances the probability of discovering vulnerabilities early before they can wreak any havoc.

Effectiveness, efficiency, longevity - these are but a few of the reasons why automated security testing is not an option for web applications, but rather a necessity.

2.4. How Does Automated Security Testing Work?

Automated security testing comprises different testing types designed to target specific vulnerabilities. These include static application security testing (SAST), dynamic application security testing (DAST), and interactive application security testing (IAST), among others.

Before deploying these tools, it's important first to identify the application's assets, design a tailored security policy based on its unique needs, create a dedicated test environment, and define clear test objectives. Once this is in place, you can let the automated security testing tools work their magic.

Such tools work by deploying various types of scans on your web application on a regular basis. These scans might search for common vulnerabilities or expose areas where your application fails to comply with specific security standards. They leverage a database that lists the latest vulnerabilities and attack vectors to effectively identify potential weaknesses in your system.

Once this scan is complete, the software will then compile a detailed report, highlighting detected vulnerabilities, their severity, and often times tips for mitigation.

2.5. Understanding Common Vulnerabilities and Exposures (CVEs)

Automated security testing tools bank significantly upon databases like the Common Vulnerabilities and Exposures (CVE) system. CVE is a list of publicly disclosed cybersecurity vulnerabilities which is crucial for maintaining updated protection strategies and effective defense mechanisms. This list plays a key role in providing standardized identifiers for said vulnerabilities.

2.6. The Importance of a Multidimensional Approach

While automation serves as a noteworthy key to efficient security practices, it is not a panacea. It needs to be coupled with regular manual testing, as human insight is necessary to contextualize potential threats. Understanding the risk a vulnerability might pose to the specific business logic or functionality of an application is something an automated tool may not perceive. Combining automated security testing with manual penetration testing offers a more holistic approach towards securing your digital assets.

Ultimately, by understanding the necessity and functionality of automated security testing, one can effectively safeguard their web resources. It's not about securing your web application today, it's about continuously protecting it for all of the tomorrows.

In the ensuing chapters, we will dive deeper into the specific types of automated security testing, how to choose the right tools, the role of a security tester, and how to effectively analyze the results from these tools. Let's start this voyage into the realm of automated security testing and pave the way for safer web applications.

Chapter 3. Understanding Web Application Vulnerabilities

Web applications, by their very nature, are exposed to a wide spectrum of threats due to their inherent accessibility. Understanding these vulnerabilities is the first step in mitigating them. This chapter will delve into the common types of web application vulnerabilities and how they can be exploited by malicious actors.

3.1. Types of Web Application Vulnerabilities and Their Exploitation

To adaptively secure our web applications, we need to comprehend the full range of vulnerabilities they could potentially operate.

1. Injection vulnerabilities Injections, like SQL, OS, and LDAP injection, are exposed when untrusted data is sent as part of a command or query. The attacker's hostile data can dupe the interpreter into executing actions or accessing unauthorized data.

2. Broken Authentication This vulnerability occurs when functions related to authentication and session management are not implemented correctly. This allows attackers to impersonate other users or even gain unauthorized access.

3. Sensitive Data Exposure At times, web applications might not adequately protect sensitive data, such as credit card numbers or authentication credentials, enabling attackers to steal or modify the data to carry out credit card fraud, identity theft, or other

kinds of crimes.

4. XML External Entity (XXE) Poorly configured XML processors can be used to expose internal files and SMB file shares or initiate remote code execution.

5. Cross-Site Scripting (XSS) In this scenario, an application includes untrusted data in a new web page without adequate validation or escaping. This permits the attacker to execute scripts in the user's browser, which can hijack user sessions or deface websites.

3.2. Mitigating Web Application Vulnerabilities

Having understood the nature and scope of potential vulnerabilities, let's now explore some of the most effective ways one can mitigate these threats.

1. Validate and Sanitize Data Data can be manipulated by an attacker, so every data input needs handling as potentially malevolent. Employ input validation to prevent improperly formed data from entering your system. Additionally, perform output encoding to protect users from malicious data.

2. Protect Cookies and Sessions Always use encrypted communication channels like HTTPS for transmitting cookies. Another good practice would be to assign a new session to each new interaction to avoid session fixation.

3. Use Web Application Firewalls WAFs could offer a decent first line of defense against web application attacks. These can help detect and mitigate various threats like DDoS, brute force attacks, and other OWASP top 10 threats.

4. Test Your Security Measures Regularly Perform regular penetration testing using automated or manual techniques. This will expose possible vulnerabilities that can be exploited by an attacker. It also helps make sure that existing security measures

function as planned.

3.3. Policy Considerations

As we carry out these protective measures, it's also essential to establish clear policies on handling web application vulnerabilities.

1. Vulnerability Disclosure Policy Sectors of policy should explicitly mention the process of reporting vulnerabilities. It should include the steps to report, who to reach out to, and the expected response times.

2. Incident Response Plan Details of swift and effective responses to confirmed security incidents ought to be included in a well-articulated plan. This includes analysis, containment, eradication, recovery, and the subsequent review.

3. Regular Staff Training Consistent and regular staff training on understanding, detecting, mitigating, and reporting vulnerabilities is a vital consideration. A team well-educated in security matters is a significant asset.

Understanding web application vulnerabilities forms the bedrock of building and maintaining a secure web application. With this insight, in addition to a combination of strategic planning, meticulous implementation, and ongoing vigilance, it's entirely possible to meet the ever-evolving cyber threats head-on and efficiently.

Chapter 4. Essentials of Security Testing: Tools and Techniques

Security Testing is an integral part of the software development cycle, aimed to ensure that the application is free from vulnerabilities and threats. Through testing, the goal is to safeguard the information from any possible breaches and protect the digital assets of an organization, thereby minimizing any potential damage to the business. This chapter delves into the intricacies of sophisticated tools and techniques, thus equipping readers with knowledge essential to the field of Security Testing.

4.1. Understanding Web Application Security

The first step in preparing for Security Testing is to understand what web application security is all about. This involves recognizing the vulnerabilities that could potentially be exploited and the repercussions of not addressing them. Security is often overlooked during the development stage, which can have serious outcomes in the future, like data breaches and system compromise. Hence, it's crucial to understand and integrate security measures right from the moment of an application's inception.

4.2. Common Web Application Vulnerabilities

To design and execute effective security testing, one should be cognizant of the common vulnerabilities that are often exploited by attackers.

1. Injection flaws, like SQL, OS, or LDAP injection: They occur when an application sends untrusted data to an interpreter.

2. Cross-Site Scripting (XSS) flaws: They happen when an application involves untrusted data in a new web page without proper validation or escaping.

3. Insecure Direct Object References: This takes place when a developer exposes a reference to an internal implementation object.

4. Security Misconfiguration: This could occur at any level of an application stack, including the platform, web server, application server, database, and framework.

5. Sensitive Data Exposure: This vulnerability exists when an application doesn't adequately protect sensitive information from being disclosed.

4.3. Tools for Web Application Security Testing

Web Application Security Testing uses specialized tools designed to detect and report vulnerabilities. They enable the structured testing of applications and provide efficient ways to discover potential threats. Some of the famous tools include:

1. OWASP ZAP: It is an open-source web application security scanner. It provides automated scanners as well as various tools that allow the cybersecurity professionals to discover security vulnerabilities.

2. Nessus: It is among the most popular vulnerability scanners. Nessus is updated daily with more than 86,000 CVEs currently in its database.

3. Burp Suite: This is an integrated platform used for attacking web applications. It contains various tools, and some of them work

together to perform a complete test.

4. Wireshark: It is a network protocol analyzer that lets you capture and interactively browse the traffic running on a computer network.

5. SQLmap: This is an open-source penetration testing tool used to automate the process of detecting and exploiting SQL injection flaws.

4.4. Techniques for Security Testing

Security testing techniques play an integral role in ensuring that the software applications are safe from any cyber threats. Various techniques include:

1. Vulnerability Scanning: This technique consists of using a computer program to scan a network or system for vulnerabilities. It includes system-level vulnerability scanning and network-level vulnerability scanning.

2. Security Scanning: It involves identifying network and system weaknesses, and later provides solutions for reducing these risks. This scanning can be performed both manually and automatically.

3. Penetration testing: This is an attempted breach of a system's security, done to reveal vulnerabilities that an adversary could exploit.

4. Risk Assessment: This involves analyzing security risks observed in the organization. Risks are classified as Low, Medium, and High.

5. Security Auditing: This is an internal inspection of Applications and Operating systems for security flaws. An audit can also be done via line by line inspection of code.

4.5. Formulating a Security Testing Strategy

Preparing for security testing involves developing a robust strategy. The following steps assist in crafting such a strategy:

1. Define the Scope: Specify the systems that need to be tested and what types of tests should be run.

2. Learn about the System: Study the system thoroughly, gather as much information as possible about the application, the network, the platform, and databases.

3. Identify Potential Threats: Based on the study, identify the various threats that may be likely to the system.

4. Prioritize Testing: After identifying the threats, prioritize them based on the risk.

5. Execute Testing: Conduct the testing based on the defined scope and tools.

6. Record and Report Results: Document every issue discovered during the testing process. Furnish sufficient details for the development team to understand the potential vulnerabilities.

4.6. Keeping up with Regulation Changes

Finally, staying updated with the changes in security regulations is equally important. As the legal landscape evolves, it's vital to maintain pace with the changing regulations to avoid any compliance issues.

In conclusion, maintaining the security of web applications is crucial in this digital age where threats are continuously evolving. Implementing comprehensive security testing practices with a structured approach or via automation can help protect our digital realm.

Chapter 5. Delving into Automated Security Testing Tools

The initial step towards understanding automated security testing tools is to figure out their context in the wider landscape of web application security. Automated testing tools can be viewed as your first line of defense, working in tandem with manual testing to identify vulnerabilities and strengthen your web application against threats. Automated tools offer several benefits such as speed of testing, consistency, wider coverage, and proficiency to execute repetitive tasks.

5.1. Understanding Automated Security Testing Tools

Automated security testing tools are applications that scan web applications for various types of security vulnerabilities. They utilize a combination of specialized algorithms, predefined security tests, and intelligent pattern matching to uncover potential weak points in the application.

There are several categories of automated testing tools:

1. Code Review Tools: These tools systematically check your code for potential security risks. They can identify bugs, deprecated functions, insecure coding practices, and other issues that may lead to a security vulnerability.

2. Web Application Security Scanners: These are specifically designed to scan web applications for common security vulnerabilities such as Cross-Site Scripting (XSS), SQL Injection, Command Injection, Path Traversal, and others.

3. Vulnerability Scanners: They scan networks and systems for known vulnerabilities. They maintain an updated database of known vulnerabilities and perform tests against your systems to see if any of them exist.

4. Penetration Testing Tools: Pen-testing tools attempt to exploit vulnerabilities in a system much like a hacker would, helping organizations understand potential real-world attack scenarios.

5.2. Choosing the Right Tool

When considering which automated security testing tool to use, several factors need to be taken into account including the cost of the tool, the skills required to utilize it, the type of vulnerabilities it can identify, the programming languages it supports, and the quality of its reports. You should assess your security needs, consider your budget, look at user reviews, and perhaps have a trial run before finally purchasing a tool.

Identifying the type of testing required is a critical step. If multiple types of scanning tests are required, it's best to go for integrated tools that offer a wide array of functions.

5.3. Most Popular Automated Security Testing Tools

Here are several commonly used tools:

1. OWASP ZAP: An open-source web app scanner developed by the Open Web Application Security Project (OWASP). ZAP is widely used for finding vulnerabilities in a web app during the development as well as testing phase.

2. Nessus: A highly popular vulnerability scanner with a loads of plugins that allow customized scanning. The tool offers a variety of scanning options, detailed reports, and more.

3. Burp Suite: A graphic tool for testing web app security, and it includes features like mapping, scanning, spidering, and more. It's highly renowned in the cybersecurity field.

4. Checkmarx: A provider of application security solutions, Checkmarx helps identify, track and fix security flaws in source codes.

5. Veracode: It allows users to scale programs and educate their developers about security vulnerabilities and their fixes during the coding process.

5.4. The advantages and disadvantages of automated security testing tools

While automated testing tools come with a myriad of advantages like fast and efficient testing, eliminating human error, ability to test large applications, they also come with limitations. These tools are not 'one size fits all' solution. They are algorithm-based, thus they lack human intuition. They might miss context-driven vulnerabilities. They cannot decipher CAPTCHA or multi-factor authentication systems. Also, a false positive can waste a lot of valuable time.

5.5. The Importance of Manual Penetration Testing

Despite all the advancements in automated security testing, we cannot discount the importance of manual penetration testing. Manual testing can understand the context, analyze complex risk scenarios, and provide a human perspective to the problem, something that automated tools simply cannot offer. Thus, it's essential to combine automated testing with manual procedures for a robust security framework.

5.6. Integrating Automated Security Tools into your SDLC

Automating security testing should penetrate all stages of your software development life cycle (SDLC), from the initial requirements analysis to the design phase, implementation, testing, deployment, and maintenance phases. Including security testing in your SDLC from the beginning can save you costs, decrease risks, and help build a solid reputation for your web application.

To conclude, automated security testing tools hold a vital place in the defense mechanism of web applications. When correctly chosen and efficiently utilized alongside manual testing procedures, they can significantly contribute to the robustness and reliability of your web application.

Chapter 6. Proactive Defense: Implementing Regular Automated Tests

In the fast-paced, continuously evolving landscape of web technology, proactive defense is not a choice but a necessity. Implementing regular automated tests is an effective strategy to achieve this objective. This process not only ensures that your applications are not vulnerable to common security attacks, but also helps you to be prepared for new threats that might emerge in the future.

6.1. Benefit of Regular Automated Tests

Automated testing comes with several advantages. First, it is an efficient way to catch vulnerabilities before malicious entities do. It also improves consistency since automated tests strictly follow the test scripts designed, thereby ensuring that no step or process is overlooked. Additionally, it provides rapid feedback to developers about the security health of their applications. As automated testing tends to be faster than manual testing, vulnerabilities can be detected earlier in the development process, making it easier and less expensive to fix.

6.2. Overview of Automated Security Testing

Automated security testing is a process where software tools are used to perform security tests automatically. These tests can be scheduled to run at regular intervals and can test different aspects of an application, such as its adherence to security requirements, its vulnerability to common exploits, and its adherence to secure coding practices. Various tools and platforms are available for this, such as OWASP ZAP, Nessus, Wireshark, and Burp Suite. Depending upon the requirements and the nature of the web applications, different tools can be employed.

6.3. Setting up a Testing Environment

Before you can start implementing regular automated tests, you'll need to set up a stable testing environment. A testing environment is a setup of software and hardware that allows you to test instances of your web application under controlled conditions. A good practice is to set up an environment that closely mirrors your production environment.

Also, remember to isolate your testing environment from your production environment to avoid accidental oversights that could lead to data leaks or breaches. Several platforms offer virtual machines and containerization technologies that can be leveraged to set up controlled, isolated environments for testing.

6.4. Implementing and Scheduling Regular Tests

Once the testing environment is set up, the next step is to implement automated security tests. To do this, you would first need to identify the security requirements for your web application. This may involve compliance requirements, business requirements, or requirements arising out of threat modeling exercises.

After the requirements are identified, you can use automated testing tools to create scripts that test these requirements. Each tool has its way of defining and configuring tests, so you would need to refer to the documentation of the specific tool you are using.

Once the scripts are prepared, you can schedule these tests to run at regular intervals. Depending on your requirements, you might want to run some tests every day, while some might be run every week or month.

As the goal is to reduce the risk of security vulnerabilities, it is beneficial to run these tests as frequently as possible. However, you also need to balance this with the computational resources these tests might consume. Hence, it's important to find a balance between security coverage and resource utilization.

6.5. Reacting to Test Results

Implementing regular automated tests is just half the battle won. The other half is about what you do with the test results. Every time automated tests run, they produce detailed reports about the health of your web application.

Test reports could include a list of vulnerabilities found, their severity, the parts of your application they affect, and suggestions for remediation. Prioritize fixing high-severity vulnerabilities which pose a bigger risk to your application. Remember, the purpose of these tests is not to simply find vulnerabilities, but also to fix them and improve overall security.

6.6. The Need for Continuous Improvement

Automated security testing is not a one-time event but a repeated process. As new threats emerge and as your application evolves, you will need to update your security requirements and test scripts. Continuously improving your automated security tests to account for these changes is a very important step in maintaining secure applications. This also includes staying up-to-date with latest methodologies and trends in automated testing, and regularly updating your software testing tools.

6.7. Conclusion

Implementing regular automated tests is a key strategy in proactive defense. It helps in identifying and rectifying vulnerabilities early, reducing the chances of security breaches dramatically. While setting up automated security testing might require initial investment in terms of time and resources, the benefits it brings in terms of application security are undoubtedly worthwhile. The truism remains relevant as ever: in web application security, the best defense is a good offense.

Chapter 7. Case Study: Success Stories of Automated Security Testing

Modern advancements in web application security have greatly benefited many companies worldwide. By adopting automated security testing, these organizations have managed to minimize potential threats, save costs, and ensure the best protection for their digital assets. In this chapter, we explore how several businesses have successfully integrated such testing into their security protocols, divulging key actions they took and the benefits they subsequently reaped.

7.1. Automating Security at Acme Corp

One of the first to embrace automated security testing was Acme Corp, a cutting-edge software development firm. Traditionally, the company relied heavily on manual security inspection; a painstaking process that ate up resources and often failed to catch sophisticated threats. Recognizing the impediments posed by this method, Acme Corp decided to transition to automated security testing.

```
[source,acme-table]
----
| Time-Period | Threats Detected (Manual) | Threats
Detected (Automated) |
| Pre-Adoption (6 months) | 200 | - |
| Post-Adoption (6 months) | - | 450 |
----
```

Table 1 clearly indicates how the transition amplified threat detection capabilities, tracking more than double the number of vulnerabilities within the same duration. Moreover, Acme also reported a 60% decrease in funds funneled into security regulation, showcasing the economic benefits of automation.

7.2. Improving Efficiency at BigSoftware Inc

BigSoftware Inc., a multinational software conglomerate, enjoyed similar successes with the adoption of automated security testing. Notorious for its diverse product range, BigSoftware was constantly bogged down by the pressure to ensure each product's security.

The burden eased once automated testing entered the scene. It standardized testing protocols across all products, upgrading the company's security software to a more advanced and time-effective version. BigSoftware also reported noticeable improvements in patching and remediation times, with issues being resolved 30% quicker than before, as shown in Table 2.

```
[source,bigsoftware-table]
----
| Period | Average Remediation Time (Days) |
| Pre-Automation | 30 |
| Post-Automation | 21 |
----
```

7.3. Cybertech Pvt Ltd: Balancing Human and Machine

At Cybertech Pvt Ltd., the focus wasn't just to replace manual practices but harmonize human expertise with automated machine efficiency. The result was a well-oiled security system adept at identifying and neutralizing a wide range of threats.

```
[source,cybertech-table]
----
| Perimeter | Threats Detected (Manual & Machine
Combined) |
| Pre-Integration | 300 |
| Post-Integration | 700 |
----
```

Table 3 underscores this hybridized approach's effectiveness, displaying a more than twofold increase in threat discovery.

7.4. Securing Startup Terrain: AlphaStart

For startup AlphaStart, automated security testing proved transformative. Despite the limited budget, the company wasn't willing to compromise on security. By shifting to a Threat Modeling tool automatically identifying design flaws and security vulnerabilities, AlphaStart could prevent potential threats without overspending, aligning their promise of robust security with smaller pockets.

```
[source,alphastart-table]
----
| Cost Component | Pre-Adoption Cost ($) | Post-Adoption
Cost ($) |
| Manpower | 20000 | 5000 |
| Software | 15000 | 7000 |
| Miscellaneous | 10000 | 5000 |
```

```
| Total | 45000 | 20000 |
----
```

Table 4 confirms significant cost savings post automation, in addition to fortifying AlphaStart's overall security stature.

These case studies reaffirm automation's promise in bolstering web application security. Whether it's enhancing threat detection like Acme Corp, streamlining operations like BigSoftware Inc, blending human-machine capabilities like Cybertech, or enabling high-quality security on a lean budget like AlphaStart; automated security testing has a role to play in all scenarios. Armed with these insights, organizations can strategize on how best to implement such technology, securing their digital futures.

Chapter 8. Walking Through Web Application Security Coding Practices

Understanding the importance of security in today's web applications is fundamental. Applications do not only provide functionality, they have also become a prime target for malicious activities. One of the key strategies to protect web applications from potential threats is by incorporating security measures right at the code level. There are several security coding practices that can be adopted to improve the overall safety of your web applications.

8.1. Why Code Secure Web Applications?

Security starts with code. Every line of code we write could potentially introduce vulnerabilities into our systems. Secure coding practices are necessary to protect the data and integrity of web applications. It mitigates threats, limits potential damage, and ensures functionality.

8.2. Secure Coding Techniques

While there are a plethora of secure coding techniques that can be used, a few key methods generally apply for most web applications. Here are some of them:

1. Input Validation: Always validate user input to ensure it's what you expect and safe before processing. Use validators that enforce correct syntax, such as RegEx for emails or phone numbers.

2. Encrypt Sensitive Information: Use encryption methods to store sensitive data like passwords, credit card numbers, and personally identifiable information (PII).

3. Least Privilege Principle: Grant users and systems the least amount of privilege they require to perform their tasks and nothing more. It minimizes the potential damage from errors or malicious activities.

4. Secure Error Handling: Implement secure error handling to prevent information leakage. Errors should not disclose sensitive information or provide clues that may aid an attacker.

8.3. Language-Specific Practices

Security coding practices may slightly vary depending on the programming language in use. Each language has its own characteristics, and it's crucial to understand how they can impact the security of your web application.

Python, for example, has been a popular choice of language for many developers and organizations. To ensure secure coding in Python, avoiding modules like 'pickle' or 'eval' that can execute arbitrary commands can protect your application from potential security risks.

JavaScript is another popular web language that requires certain precautions. It's important to properly handle the cross-origin resource sharing (CORS) settings and keep the client-side secure against Cross-Site Scripting (XSS) by implementing Content Security Policies (CSP).

8.4. Building Security Touchpoints

To achieve maximum security levels, building security touchpoints throughout the development lifecycle is key. These touchpoints ensure that security is not an afterthought but an integral part of the development process. These touchpoints include:

1. Requirements: Mentioning security requirements along with functional requirements encourages developers to consider security from the start.

2. Design: Documenting how the software will meet all the security requirements in the design specification ensures it's planned out before development begins.

3. Implementation: Incorporating the secure coding practices as discussed above during this stage.

4. Verification: Using tools like static application security testing (SAST) or dynamic application security testing (DAST) to identify vulnerabilities.

5. Release: Following the secure release management procedures to ensure secure deployment of the application.

8.5. Awareness and Training

The landscape of web application security is continuously evolving, and threats are becoming increasingly sophisticated. Constant learning and the ability to adapt to new situations are prerequisites for coding securely. Developer teams should regularly update their skills and knowledge about emerging threats and the corresponding preventive measures.

In conclusion, writing secure code is not only the responsibility of the individual coder, but of the whole team, project managers, and decision-makers involved in the development process. It needs collective efforts to adopt best practices for secure coding. By reading this chapter, you've taken a meaningful step towards reinforcing the security of your web application. Keep going, and remember: in web application security, every line of code counts.

Chapter 9. Threat Modelling: Anticipating Cybersecurity Challenges

To counteract the ever-evolving cyber threats, anticipating potential cybersecurity challenges is a fundamental initial step. This chapter highlights what threat modeling is, why it is essential, and how it plays a crucial role in identifying and mitigating possible threats before they manifest into significant cybersecurity issues.

Chapter 10. Overview of Threat Modeling

Threat modeling is a systematic process that enables organizations to identify, manage, and potentially eliminate security threats. It allows for the comprehensive evaluation of potential vulnerabilities and ensures that they are addressed during the design and development stages, rather than after deployment when the damage can be significantly greater.

Threat modeling involves identifying potential threats and creating solutions for those threats. It evolves to mirror the changing threat landscape, ensuring that as new threats are recognized, they can be promptly and effectively mitigated.

10.1. Threat Modeling Process

There are four standard steps involved in the threat modeling process:

1. Define the scope: Initially, define the application or system being modeled.

2. Create a detailed architectural diagram: This multifaceted diagram should comprise of data flows, interfaces, trust boundaries, and components.

3. Identify potential threats: With this structure, the next step is to find the possible threats within each component and flow.

4. Mitigate identified threats: After identifying potential threats, the final task is to find ways to prevent or mitigate each one.

This cyclical process ensures that your system is continually updated and prepared for the evolving threat landscape.

10.2. Advantages of Threat Modeling

Threat modeling provides organizations with a range of benefits. These include:

1. It exposes potential security threats early, allowing mitigation strategies to be put in place before threats cause harm.

2. The structured process facilitates improved communication between different teams, ensuring a comprehensive and unified security approach.

3. Threat modeling helps in prioritizing security tasks by making apparent the most critical threats first.

4. It promotes proactive rather than reactive security.

Chapter 11. Steps in Threat Modeling

11.1. Identify Security Objectives

Security objectives are the foundation of an efficient threat modeling process. Recognizing what you need to protect helps determine the potential threats against the same comprehensively. Security objectives can range from protecting sensitive customer data to maintaining the system's uptime.

11.2. Create a Detailed Application Overview

Once you understand what needs to be secured, the next step is to build a detailed application overview. This process involves creating system diagrams that accurately represent all the elements involved, including subsystems, data flows, and trust boundaries.

It is important to document and understand:

1. Private and public parts of the application.

2. How the application interacts with other systems.

3. Where and how user data is stored and processed.

4. Authentication and access controls in place.

Understanding these elements can help you discern the areas most vulnerable to an attack.

11.3. Identify and Analyze Threats

With an understanding of the system architecture and data flow, you can begin to identify potential threats. Some commonly applied approaches for this step include:

1. STRIDE: A threat classification model developed by Microsoft, standing for Spoofing, Tampering, Repudiation, Information Disclosure, Denial of Service, and Elevation of Privilege.

2. PASTA: Process for Attack Simulation and Threat Analysis is a risk-based threat modeling framework focusing on business objectives.

Threats can be categorized based on their intent, methods, impact, and other similar factors.

11.4. Prioritize and Respond to Threats

After the identification of potential threats, the next step is threat prioritization. Prioritization primarily depends upon the severity and impact of the threat, ease of exploitation, and the value of the asset at risk. Some commonly used models for threat prioritization are CVSS (Common Vulnerability Scoring System) and DREAD (Damage potential, Reproducibility, Exploitability, Affected users, and Discoverability).

Even though it is not feasible to address all threats simultaneously, prioritization allows stakeholders to focus on severe threats immediately while planning for less serious threats.

11.5. Validate, Monitor, and Iterate

Once identified threats are mitigated, it is crucial to validate the effectiveness of the mitigation strategies. Adopting a monitoring system to detect when the instantiated security measures fail is also crucial. Threat modeling is an iterative process that requires you to continuously review the model, making alterations and updates whenever necessary.

Chapter 12. Threat Modeling Tools

Several automated threat modeling tools can enhance the efficiency and precision of the process. Microsoft's Threat Modeling Tool, OWASP Threat Dragon, and securiCAD are a few notable examples. These tools can greatly assist in the visualization, identification, and mitigation of potential threats.

Chapter 13. Conclusion

While threat modeling can seem like a daunting task, it is an invaluable tool for anticipating and preparing for cybersecurity challenges. Detailed threat modeling allows us to envision possible threats before they form and strategize ways to prevent or diminish their potential impact. Regardless of its complexity, threat modeling should be key in the design and development processes of any web application or system. By integrating threat modeling into daily processes, organizations can ensure they are ready for not just today's threats but future ones as well.

Remember, in cybersecurity, being proactive is always better than being reactive. Threat modeling provides us just that initiative by enabling us to anticipate potential threats and strategize on how best to mitigate them.

Chapter 14. From Reactive to Proactive: Developing an Effective Security Testing Strategy

A shift towards a proactive approach in security is not only beneficial but crucial in the long run. Historically, security has often been reactive, addressing issues as they arise. However, as the cyber landscape evolves and becomes increasingly volatile, a proactive approach to security testing is vital.

The nature of cyber-attacks is morphing at an exponential rate. Hackers are devising new strategies and exploiting vulnerabilities faster than ever. It's no longer sufficient to address security weaknesses retrospectively. We need to anticipate, prepare, and prevent.

14.1. The Proactive Approach: A Paradigm Shift

Going proactive implies a paradigm change in how we handle security. From patching up vulnerabilities as they surface, we transition to anticipating potential weaknesses and fortifying them before attackers can exploit them.

Proactive security testing leverages automated tools to scan and test your application for potential vulnerabilities during development rather than waiting until it's in production. It creates feedback loops that allow continuous improvement and fortification of your digital assets.

14.2. The Merits of Proactive Testing

Being proactive grants you several benefits.

The adage, "prevention is better than cure," aligns perfectly with proactive security. When vulnerabilities are not accounted for during the development process, the expenses and repercussions of remediation could be monumental — not only in financial terms but also in terms of trust and customer relationships.

Having a step ahead of attackers is always beneficial, and this strategy offers exactly that. By identifying potential weaknesses ahead of time, you prevent your application from being the low-hanging fruit attackers generally pursue.

14.3. The Reactive Method: A Study

The reactive method, while still prevalent and necessary in some cases, carries multiple pitfalls.

Primarily, this approach opens up an opportunity window for hackers to exploit any unattended vulnerabilities between the discovery and fixing times. This reactive window can have disastrous impacts, attributing to data breach or system compromise scenarios.

Additionally, reactive testing often leads to 'patchwork' fixes, which could create complex dependencies and even new vulnerabilities.

14.4. Leveraging Automated Tools for Proactive Security

Automated security testing plays a pivotal role in transitioning from a reactive security testing approach to a proactive one.

Tools like static application security testing (SAST) and dynamic application security testing (DAST) can be employed during the development process to identify vulnerabilities. While SAST looks at source code for potential vulnerabilities, DAST behaves like an outsider attacking the application looking for weak points.

These tools factor into the Continuous Integration/Continuous Deployment (CI/CD) pipeline, ensuring a constant feedback loop for developers to address the vulnerabilities in real-time.

14.5. Develop a Risk-Based Strategy

Not every risk is equal, and it's crucial to gauge the potential impact of a risk. A risk-based strategy can help prioritize efforts towards vulnerabilities that have the most substantial impact, considering factors like potential financial loss, reputational damage, or even legal implications.

Implement risk assessment tools to prioritize risks, ranking them based on severity.

14.6. Cultivate an Organizational Culture around Proactive Security

Attaining a proactive security posture is not merely about employing advanced tools or developing robust strategies. It's equally about cultivating an organizational culture that values security.

Develop a security-aware environment right from your developers to your top-level management. Regular training, workshops, and security drills can foster this environment. A collective participation and appreciation of security can drive substantive improvements.

14.7. Integrating Security into the Development Lifecycle

Infuse security at every step of the software development lifecycle (SDLC). Instead of treating security as an afterthought, security measures should be an integral part of design, development, testing, and deployment phases.

Tools like Security Requirements Traceability Matrix (SRTM) can help you ensure that the security requirements are met at every stage of SDLC.

14.8. Continual Learning and Improvement

The world of cybersecurity is continually evolving. What works today might not be as effective tomorrow. Therefore, continually learning, adapting, and improving must be the crux of an effective proactive security testing strategy.

Prioritize security reviews, engage in 'red teaming', where a group acts as potential hackers to find vulnerabilities, and stay current with latest security practices and trends.

14.9. Conclusion

Transitioning from a reactive to a proactive approach requires an acknowledgment of the changing cybersecurity landscape. It demands a systemic shift, the integration of automated tools, the cultivation of a security-conscious culture, and a thirst for continual learning and enhancement.

In an age where threats are increasingly agile, "the best defense is a good offense." A proactive security testing strategy ensures that your offense is robust and agile. By highlighting potential weaknesses before an attacker can exploit them, we can mitigate the risks and continually safeguard our digital assets.

The shift may be demanding, but the dividends— in the form of peace of mind, customer trust, and financial protection— are invaluable. By incorporating these steps into your security posture, you can make the shift from reactive to proactive security, securing not just today but the many tomorrows to come.

Chapter 15. Future Trends in Automated Security Testing

With emerging trends in the digital landscape, it is essential to stay abreast of the key game-changing elements to maintain robust security protocols. This chapter delves into the future trends in automated security testing.

15.1. The Surge of AI and Machine Learning

Artificial Intelligence and Machine Learning are set to revolutionize industry aspects, and automated security testing is no exception. AI/ML algorithms can learn from past incidents and predict potential breaches, thereby enhancing security robustness.

Machine learning models build on patterns derived from historical data, which allows them to predict suspicious activities or anomalies accurately. In contrast, AI simulates human intelligence to perform complex tasks, like identifying evolving threats in real-time. Together, these technologies promise more advanced automated security testing tools capable of not just identifying existing vulnerabilities but also predicting potential threats.

15.2. Continuous and Comprehensive Testing

Continuous, comprehensive security testing is another significant trend shaping the future of automated security testing. As DevOps continues to console development and operations, the need for continuous testing grows. This trend points towards the incorporation of testing in every phase of the development cycle, resulting in the DevSecOps - integrating security into DevOps.

Continuous testing allows for instant detection and resolution of security issues, reducing the time and costs involved with traditional staged security testing. Further, this automates monitoring to detect vulnerabilities in live applications, enabling prompt responses to live threats.

15.3. Integration of Tools

IT teams no longer function in isolated silos; today's solutions call for integration across all platforms. Future trends point towards integrated toolsets capable of managing and automating security testing actions.

Such integrated tools will offer multi-faceted security solutions and the ability to seamlessly collaborate with other tools to solve complex security problems. Tighter integration between security tools and project management or bug tracking tools will streamline vulnerability management, reducing the risk of overlooked issues.

15.4. Increased Usage of Blockchain

Blockchain has now moved beyond the realm of cryptocurrency, finding relevance in securing web applications. It offers a decentralized approach to storing data, making it tamper-proof and highly reliable.

In terms of security testing, blockchain technology can provide an immutable record of all testing activities, including identified threats, conducted tests, and the measures taken to mitigate potential risks. This impact extends to automated security testing, which can leverage the blockchain to verify and validate test data.

15.5. Rise of User Behavior Analytics

User Behavior Analytics (UBA) is gaining traction, providing a sophisticated approach to identifying potential risks based on user activities. Automated security testing tools will increasingly incorporate UBA features that analyze behavioral patterns to pinpoint anomalies and potential threats.

From studying historical user behavior to establishing what qualifies as 'normal' behavior, these tools can flag deviations that may signify a security risk. This approach permits proactive security measures, ensuring that system vulnerabilities are addressed before they can be exploited.

15.6. The Evolution of Risk-Based Testing

Risk-Based Testing (RBT) helps prioritize testing activities based on the level of risk associated with each vulnerability. This cost-effective approach ensures high-risk areas receive the greatest focus. Future automated security testing tools will likely factor in risk levels more comprehensively, applying AI algorithms to accurately forecast risk and direct testing efforts accordingly.

Evidently, a wave of innovation is poised to navigate automated security testing towards more advanced, accurate, and efficient horizons. By understanding these trends, stakeholders can equip themselves better to protect their web applications in this ever-dynamic landscape. As technology evolves, so too will the tools we use, ushering in a new era of sophisticated, automated security testing.

www.ingramcontent.com/pod-product-compliance
Lightning Source LLC
LaVergne TN
LVHW051623050326
832903LV00033B/4634